NEGOTIATE TO WIN!
THE INTRODUCTORY EDITION

Ian Moncrief-Scott

Information Management Solutions Limited

ISLE OF MAN

The author Ian Moncrief-Scott has asserted his right under the Copyright, Designs and Patents Act 1988 to be identified as the author of this work.

Copyright. © I. Moncrief-Scott 2021

All rights reserved. No part of this publication may be produced in any form or by any means - graphic, electronic, or mechanical, including photocopying, recording, taping, or information storage and retrieval systems - without the prior permission in writing of the publishers.

The publishers make no representation, express or implied, regarding the accuracy of the information contained in this book and cannot accept any legal responsibility for any errors or omissions that may take place.

A CIP catalogue record for this book is available from the British Library.

Published by Information Management Solutions Limited, 17 Howe Road, Onchan, Isle of Man, IM3 2BB.

Printed, bound and distributed by IngramSpark.

Book Layout © 2017 BookDesignTemplates.com

Cover Source by Tanja Prokop of BookDesignTemplates.com

NEGOTIATE TO WIN!: THE INTRODUCTORY EDITION – 2nd ed.
ISBN 9781903467190

The Publishers have been requested by the author to acknowledge the direct and indirect contributions to this book by:

The author's parents, who gave him the chance to learn, teach and share.

Tom Norman
Tom Campbell
Eddy Campbell
Bill Leach
Mike Mairone
English Electric Co Ltd
R R Donnelley & Sons (Chicago)
Tillotsons Ltd

This book is dedicated to
start-up entrepreneurs.

The front cover depicts
ordinary wooden clothes pegs dressed as
Super Heroes.

**All start-up entrepreneurs are
ordinary people
turning into Super Heroes!**

CONTENTS

INTRODUCTION	1
PLANNING	5
LISTENING	7
TALKING	9
TIPPING THE BALANCE	11
FINAL THOUGHT	13
OTHER BOOKS BY THE AUTHOR (Print)	15
OTHER BOOKS BY THE AUTHOR (eBook)	17
NEW EDITIONS & FORTHCOMING BOOKS BY THE AUTHOR	19

CHAPTER ONE

INTRODUCTION

For many people negotiating is simply taking cash to their local garage and getting something off the showroom price. Others think that using a potential supplier's quotation to pressure an existing vendor to cut prices is professional negotiation.

Some believe it is a power moment. Another view would be convincing your daughter that if she saves her pocket money you will double it so she can have that new dress.

Years ago, I was asked to describe what was meant by negotiation. I repeated the mistakes made by most. Explanations like 'meeting mutual objectives through bargaining', 'holding discussions to find corporate symmetry', expressing a requirement and hammering out a deal.'

Very simply, negotiation is:

    PLANNING - LISTENING - TALKING.

Much is made of statements like *Win - Win*, *Cutting a Deal* and *Drilling Down into Cost Issues*. These are what they purport to be – statements. This is not negotiating, only a minor representation of the bargaining process.

Real negotiation is much more sophisticated. You prepare. You question. You observe. You deploy. You execute. Effective negotiating is achieved by planning, listening and talking. '*Negotiating to Win*' amplifies that process to tip the balance in your favour.

Everyone wants something for nothing. Human nature. A bargain. That's why lotteries, car boots, fairs and scams are so successful. This book gives you something for nothing. Other than the cover price, it's free. You do not require lotions, potions, investment, expenditure and complex tactics. All you have to grasp are simple techniques that you can refine at your own pace to meet your own needs.

Politicians might be shocked by extent that effective negotiation can have on the nation's balance of payments and environmentalists may be stunned by the impact on natural resources.

The approaches I have presented apply to any type of negotiation involving any product and service.

I was fortunate to be blessed with some natural negotiating ability. I did not realise it until well into my career. Reading business books and attending training courses made me see that I had skills that others had not.

Most courses and books concentrate on tactics and strategies instead of stressing the vital importance of the STAGES of negotiation. They expound bluff and double bluff. Complex theories. Ponderous phrases. Buzz words.

CHAPTER TWO

PLANNING

What is negotiating? Sitting at a table and bargaining with someone? No.

Before you sit down, pick up a telephone phone or write a letter. You must prepare and plan. Why? I don't have time. Things have to be done there and then.

Preparation is paramount. If you have not prepared, how can you measure what you are asking and receiving are correct.

Many buyers say, "The supplier has a price list or the store has put a nice sign on top of the refrigerator which says £199. The price is not negotiable."

I reply, "What gave him the right to set your mutual price? What about all the other factors, delivery, warranty, extras, etc.?"

In the Western world, we have been conditioned to think of the other side. *Win/Win* is a classic example. Buyers and sellers often come to me and say, "I want to learn how to conduct *Win/Win* deals."

My response is, "What do you mean?" The inevitable response is, "I want to make sure that the other party and myself are both satisfied."

I ask, "Why? How do you measure *Win/Win*? How do you know the other party is satisfied or not? Because he tells you he is? Can you rely on that?"

Let me make one important point. I detest unethical methods and tactics. You must treat all proponents with the highest standards of integrity and honesty, even if they do not reciprocate.

I always say to negotiators, "Forget about what you perceive as the other party's needs. Your job is to get the deal that you decide you can justify. Establish your need and persuade the other party to provide it. Don't worry about your opponent. Let him handle his position and you concentrate on yours."

"What happens if I put him out of business and lose my supplier or customer?" That should not happen if you have conducted your side of the negotiations properly. You should know if you are going to put him out of business as you should be as equally aware you will not.

CHAPTER THREE

LISTENING

My wife is a great listener. She is arguably the best listener I have ever encountered, an absolute natural. When all around are losing their heads, she has the knack of listening intently to what people are really saying. She can divorce the emotion from fact and need. It is a gift, but you can learn it as well.

Why is listening so important? If you are listening you are not speaking. If you are silent, you are not imparting information. Leading textbooks all expound 'Information is Power!' Without information we are blind and lost. With it we can find our way.

This applies to negotiation. To make judgements you need information. You cannot gain detailed knowledge without listening to what is being said.

You must also be careful when listening that you are not just hearing as an interlude to speaking again. Listen carefully to what is being said. How is the information being portrayed and conveyed?

Many people cannot listen effectively.

To listen intently is very difficult, especially if you are under pressure and concentrating on what you are going to say next. If necessary, use a colleague whose sole task is to monitor precisely what the other party is saying and act on the information received.

CHAPTER FOUR

TALKING

Why talk? To exercise your vocal chords or expound great theories? Talking is almost as important as listening. More important, some would contend. The right kind of talking is vital. Wrong kinds can be disastrous.

There are two points to understand when talking. Firstly, you are giving information. Be sure that this is information you want and intend to give. Remember the war adage, 'careless talk cost lives.'

Secondly, when you talk, ask questions. These come in two forms. Open and closed.

An example of a closed question - Do you feel that your price reflects the market? This begs the answer yes or no! You could receive no more details than that.

An open question solicits information: How have you established your price? The respondent must provide details or risk losing the initiative. Get used to using information-hungry questions and making best use of What, How, Where, Why, Who.

CHAPTER FIVE

TIPPING THE BALANCE

How can you achieve this?

Imagine a pair of scales. They are in equilibrium. You take the left-hand position. Your opponent assumes the right.

There are two ways the balance arm can move - upwards and downwards. If your side moves upwards, you are losing your advantage. If your side goes downwards, you are gaining weight and thereby advantage.

To make the arm move you attach weights. These can be large or small, to represent important and less valuable points. The weights can be fixed on the top of the arm, in a positive way or beneath in a negative manner.

The same can be said of the arguments they represent. You can coerce your opponent with statements like 'take it or leave it' (negative) or by logical persuasion (positive).

Proper planning will determine size of the weights, and when and where to place them.

CHAPTER SIX

FINAL THOUGHT

I hope that this outline has whetted your appetite. You have already learned the basic principles. *Negotiate to Win* is an approach not a tactic. Success is there for the taking. You already have a better position that you imagine. Don't lose it!

Tip the balance before the other party seizes the initiative.

Look out for

Negotiate to Win!
The Full Edition.

OTHER BOOKS BY THE AUTHOR (Print)

As Good As Gold. ISBN 0-9534818-4-0

Currants, Olives & Cotton. ISBN 99781903467077

De La Rue Straw Hats to Global Securities. ISBN 0- 9534818-2-4
De La Rue: Straw Hats to Global Securities. ISBN 9781903467046

Euro History & Development. ISBN 0-9534818-1-6
Euro: History & Development. ISBN 9781903467053

Holidays 2000. ISBN 0-9534818-7-5

Negotiate to Win! ISBN 0-9534818-6-7

Start Any Business. ISBN 9781903467008

Scripophily. ISBN 0-9534818-5-9
Scripophily. ISBN 9781903467084

Tail-less Cats & Three-Legged Men. ISBN 9781903467091

The Eternal Old Lady. ISBN 0-9534818-3-2
The Eternal Old Lady ISBN 9781903467060

The Green Shoots of Money. ISBN 9781903467107

The Hitmen - Part One. ISBN 0-9534818-8-3

OTHER BOOKS BY THE AUTHOR (eBook)

As Good As Gold. ISBN 9781903467121

Currants, Olives & Cotton. ISBN 9781903467169

De La Rue. ISBN 9781903467138

Euro. ISBN 9781903467145

Start Any Business. ISBN 9781903467015

Scripophily. ISBN 9781903467176

Tail-less Cats & Three-legged Men. ISBN 9781903467183

The Eternal Old Lady. ISBN 9781903467152

The Green Shoots of Money. ISBN 9781903467114

NEW EDITIONS & FORTHCOMING BOOKS BY THE AUTHOR

Holidays 2000 (Print). ISBN 9781903467213
Holidays 2000 (eBook). ISBN 9781903467220

ABOUT THE AUTHOR

Ian Moncrief-Scott has over fifty years of broad business experience, mostly gained at international level, based in the UK.

As a former senior executive for a global publishing and information technology company headquartered in the USA, he has contributed to numerous client-facing procurement and outsourcing initiatives worldwide.

Ian has created and participated in numerous small businesses in the UK, Isle of Man and elsewhere.

He has also represented the Isle of Man Government Department for Enterprise in several of its business support schemes. Ian designed and delivered extensive training for its Micro Business Grant Scheme.

In recognition of his long-term service to the Department, Ian was nominated for The Queen's Award for Enterprise Promotion and awarded an official Certificate of Recognition in 2018.

Throughout his career, he has maintained an active interest in start-ups, especially those involving the financial sector.

www.ingramcontent.com/pod-product-compliance
Lightning Source LLC
Chambersburg PA
CBHW071551080526
44588CB00011B/1868